AUTHOR

Gabriele Malavoglia was born in Milan in 1989. After completing his high school studies, he moved to Spain to pursue his university studies, remaining on Iberian soil after graduation. Passionate since childhood about Italian and Spanish Military History, he is a self-taught scholar and is taking his first steps in the field of editorialism. He lives in Zaragoza and works as a logistics consultant for some local companies.

PUBLISHING'S NOTES

None of unpublished images or text of our book may be reproduced in any format without the expressed written permission of Luca Cristini Editore (already Soldiershop.com) when not indicate as marked with license creative commons 3.0 or 4.0. Luca Cristini Editore has made every reasonable effort to locate, contact and acknowledge rights holders and to correctly apply terms and conditions to Content.

Every effort has been made to trace the copyright of all the photographs. If there are unintentional omissions, please contact the publisher in writing at: info@soldiershop.com, who will correct all subsequent editions.

Our trademark: Luca Cristini Editore©, and the names of our series & brand: Soldiershop, Witness to war, Museum book, Bookmoon, Soldiers&Weapons, Battlefield, War in colour, Historical Biographies, Darwin's view, Fabula, Altrastoria, Italia Storica Ebook, Witness To History, Soldiers, Weapons & Uniforms, Storia etc. are herein © by Luca Cristini Editore.

LICENSES COMMONS

This book may utilize part of material marked with license creative commons 3.0 or 4.0 (CC BY 4.0), (CC BY-ND 4.0), (CC BY-SA 4.0) or (CC0 1.0). We give appropriate attribution credit and indicate if change were made in the acknowledgments field. Our WTW books series utilize only fonts licensed under the SIL Open Font License or other free use license.

For a complete list of Soldiershop titles please contact Luca Cristini Editore on our website: www.soldiershop.com or www.cristinieditore.com. E-mail: info@soldiershop.com

Title: **TANKS OF THE SPANISH CIVIL WAR** Code.: **WTW-038 EN** by Gabriele Malavoglia
ISBN code: 978-88-93279017 Forst edition October 2022
Text: English Nr. of images: 154 layout: 177,8x254mm Cover & Art Design: Luca S. Cristini

WITNESS TO WAR (SOLDIERSHOP) is a trademark of Luca Cristini Editore, via Orio, 35/4 - 24050 Zanica (BG) ITALY.

WITNESS TO WAR

TANKS OF THE SPANISH CIVIL WAR
ARMOURED UNITS

PHOTOS & IMAGES FROM WORLD WARTIME ARCHIVES

GABRIELE MALAVOGLIA

BOOKS TO COLLECT

Contents

Introduction..5
    The preludes of the Spanish Civil War..5
    Spain catches fire...5
    Tanks come into play...5

Nationalist Armoured Units...7
    Spanish Armoured Units...7
    Italian Armoured Units...21
    German Armoured Units...45

Republican Armoured Units...65

Bibliography..96

Acnkowledgements...98

▲ A Spanish Schneider CA-1 tank, photographed during the Rif War (1921 - 1926), which was the baptism of fire of the Iberian armoured units.

INTRODUCTION

The preludes of the Spanish Civil War

In Spain, after the ousting of the Dictator Miguel Primo de Rivera in 1930, radical Republicans seized power in 1931, forcing King Alfonso XIII to leave the country and declaring the Republic constituted.

The social, political and economic tensions that had been created were exacerbated by attempts to take liberalism (by the centrists) and socialism (by the left) to extremes, which led to the emergence of a reactionary right wing.

The left Republican factions, although supporting the common cause of the Republic, were not really united due to significant ideological differences, just as they were divided by the other centrist Republican parties. The use of the term 'Republican' during the Civil War did not, in fact, denote any real ideological unity beyond the fight against the Nationalists.

The Right was made up of monarchists, fascists, Catholics and conservatives, who, although they did not identify themselves as a united political force, joined forces closely due to the repression of the Republicans and arrived at the outbreak of war stronger.

The unity of the Republic was also put to the test by the separatist movements in Catalonia and the Basque Country; in the latter region, the left-wing movement was very powerful, especially the CNT (Confederacion Nacional de Trabajo) trade union and the anarchists of the FAI (Federaciôn Anarquista ibérica).

The tensions between the factions of the Republicans grew steadily, causing the failure of the project to modernise the country, which caused discontent in much of Spanish society, and which in turn led to the victory of the centre-right coalition in the 1933 elections. The Republicans and the left refused to accept the result. The elections of 1933 had major repercussions in the military, as the army was practically purged by the Republicans, the economy causing a reduction of farmers' wages and, consequently, the social spheres typified by the miners' strike in Asturias in 1934, which was bloodily repressed by Francisco Franco, and resulted in the death of at least 1,700 miners and the arrest of between 15,000 and 30,000.

New elections in early 1936 were called after the collapse of the government, which again gave the Republicans a majority, while tensions within the country were now uncontrollable.

Spain catches fire

Civil war broke out in July 1936, but the plans had been developed over previous months, with the hope of a quick overthrow of the unstable Republican government. A coup d'état broke out in the Spanish territories of Morocco and some cities in southern Spain, but the hope for a quick resolution of the revolt quickly vanished. On the one hand, the Nationalists failed to gain much ground beyond the southern part of the country, on the other hand, the Republicans reacted and organised themselves very slowly.

The Nationalists received the full support of the fascists in Italy and from the National Socialists ruling in Germany, while the Republicans, due to a lack of weapons, ammunition and logistical organisation, found it difficult to defend themselves against the advancing rebel forces.

Tanks come into play

The Spanish Civil War was the first conflict to see clashes between tanks, employed by both sides, in fact, at the same time, Italy was fighting in Ethiopia, employing a good number of armoured vehicles, but the clash was against an enemy that was completely without tanks.

Let us take a step back to analyse the development of armoured vehicles in Spain. The first tank acquired by Alfonso XIII's Spain was a Renault FT-17, which arrived in Madrid on 23 June 1919. The vehicle underwent a series of tests at the Carabanchel Central Artillery School in Madrid, experiments that led to the replacement of the original armament with a 7 mm machine gun. The FT-17 tanks acquired, together with half a dozen Schneider CA-1 assault tanks, formed the backbone of the Spanish Army's nascent armoured units.

The baptism of fire of the Spanish tanks took place in Morocco during the Rif War which was rather disastrous as during the Battle of Anoual in July 1921, the Spanish had lost more than 12,000 men. Consequently, modernisation programmes were initiated, which led to the creation of the FT-17 Assault Tank Company of eleven tanks on 17 December 1921. On 9 March 1922, the first tank unit of the Spanish Army was officially created in response to the request of the General Staff to increase the firepower of the units engaged in the Rif War. The unit had its baptism of fire on 14 March 1922, two days after their landing in Morocco, proving to be a valuable support during the operations carried out by the Spanish infantry; a few years later these

tanks participated in the first amphibious operation by landing at Al Hoceima on 9 September 1925. The Rif War gave Spanish forces the first opportunity to test armoured vehicles in combat and develop tactics.

Starting in 1923, the Army acquired more Renault FT-17s and Schneider CA-1s; an Italian Fiat 3000-A tank was also purchased, with the aim of evaluating its performance, and the study of a domestically produced tank, the Trubia, to be manufactured in the factory in the Asturian town of the same name, was begun. This tank was superior to its French peers in terms of armament and engine performance, but the Spanish industry was unable to mass-produce it.

There was, however, ample availability of protected trucks, basically with the addition of steel plates for protection, the disadvantage of the vehicles though was their considerable size being almost 6 metres long, 4 metres high and more than 2 metres wide, and with excessive weight at around 6,000 kilograms together with a fairly high centre of gravity, which increased the risk of tipping over in battle.

At the beginning of the Civil War, the Spanish Army had a total of 15 FT-17s, a single Fiat 3000-A, 6 Schneider CA1 assault tanks, 4 Trubia tanks, 2 Landesa tanks and 46 Bilbao armoured cars.

Soon afterwards, Spain became the testing ground for modern armoured warfare, but not so much for the existing tanks, but for those sent to Italy from Germany and Russia. The use of tanks during the Civil War gave a glimpse to some of those aspects that would later make armoured forces one of the decisive elements on the battlefield during the Second World War. In Spain, not only the different technologies and conceptions of armoured vehicles clashed, but also the different schools of thought of the time: that of Fuller and Liddell Hart of Great Britain, that of Soviet Marshal Tukhachesvkii and that of the 'Lightning War' of German Colonel Guderian.

Although they took an active part in the Spanish conflict, the Italian Carristi had very different experiences from those of their counterparts in other countries, especially because Italian armoured units were always employed in an extremely restricted manner, principally as support for Infantry operations.

On the whole, the Italian and German tanks demonstrated their limitations against the Soviet armoured tanks in terms of firepower. But while the Germans could rely on their special 7.92mm armour-piercing ammunition, the Italian Carristi had to rely on flame-throwing fast tanks in close and extremely dangerous combat in order to hope to overcome the Soviet-made tanks.

NATIONALIST ARMOURED UNITS

Spanish armoured units

Almost all the armoured equipment available in Spain at the outbreak of the Civil War ended up in the hands of the Republican troops, with the exception of 6 Renault FT17 tanks (5 according to other sources) of the Regimiento Ligero de Carros de Combate No. 2 from Zaragoza, 2 Schneider CA1s, 3 Trubia tanks from Oviedo and 5 Bilbao armoured cars.

The Renault tanks of the Zaragoza Regiment initially joined the so-called 'Mobile Column' or 'Blasco Column' organised by General Cabanillas to support the national positions around Zaragoza, being destroyed in combat over the following months. The Tank Company effectively disbanded at the end of July, when 3 tanks were returned to Zaragoza, while a section of 2 tanks was sent to Somosierra, where they fought against enemy armoured units.

With the numerous FT17s captured during the Northern campaign, the Nationalists formed the 6th Company of the Batallón de Carros de Combate in February 1937, which was seldom used in combat; in March 1938 it was re-equipped with T-26Bs and the FT-17 tanks were sent to the Escuela de Carros.

In September 1936, the Base de Carros del Ejército Nacional was established near Cáceres, to which the German advisers and instructors of Panzergruppe 'Thoma' were assigned. In fact, the Panzergruppe only had training tasks and the Germans transformed the Regimiento de Infanteria Argel No. 37 into the 1st Battallon da Carros de Combate, articulated on:

- 1st Company with 16 tanks (3 Sections each with 5 tanks plus 1 command tank)
- 2nd Company with 16 tanks (3 Sections each with 5 tanks plus 1 command tank)
- 3rd Company with 16 tanks (3 Sections each with 5 tanks plus 1 command tank), formed in November with the Panzer I B tanks that had just arrived from Germany
- Anti-tank gun company (2 Sections of 4 Pak 35/37 37 mm, towed by Krupp L-2 H43 Protze tractors)
- Transport company
- Workshop

It was based in Cubas de la Sagra, near Madrid.

With Bilbao armoured cars captured from the Republicans in Toledo in September 1936, the 'Compañía de Carros Blindados' was created at the end of the month in two sections, which, until 1937, acted as a training unit for Spanish armoured troops, including five Bilbaos modified with flamethrowers instead of machine guns, called Bilbao 'Lanzallamas'. This company was also sent to Madrid, in support of the columns that were besieging the capital. Two Bilbao "Lanzallamas" were left at the castle of Las Arguijuelas, where the first base of the armoured detachment of the Condor Legion in Spain was located; while the other three "Lanzallamas" were sent to the front of Talavera on 26 October 1936.

In August 1937, a new shipment of 30 Panzer I A's replaced the losses and created the 4th Tank Company. Later the Battalion was reorganised as a Mixed Battalion on:

- 4 Companies equipped with 'Negrillos'
- 1 Company armed with Soviet vehicles
- 1 Motorised Anti-Tank Company
- 1 Logistics Company

On 1 October 1937, the Battalion was divided into two Groups, each equipped with a command tank, two Panzer I Tank Companies and one T-26B Tank Company (the two Companies armed with Russian tanks were the 5th and 6th).

On 1 March 1938, the Tank Battalion became part of the Legión, with the name 'Bandera de Carros de Combate de la Legión', maintaining the same structure, with the addition of a 7th Company, equipped with Renault FT-17s, with training functions.

In October 1938, the Bandera was renamed the Agrupación de Carros de Combate de la Legión, structured into two Battalions: the first with three Companies (called by the Spanish "1st Group of the Bandera de Carros de Combate"), and the second ("2nd Group of the Bandera de Carros de Combate") with two Companies which became three in January 1939 with the addition of a T-26B Company. Each Company, was equipped with both German and Soviet tanks and therefore called 'Negrillos y Russos', was formed as follows:

- Command Platoon (1 Panzer I tank, 2 motorcycles, 1 light truck)
- 1st Platoon (1 T-26B tank, 4 Panzer I tanks)
- 2nd Platoon (1 T-26B tank, 4 Panzer I tanks)
- 3rd Platoon (1 T-26B tank, 4 Panzer I tanks then, from 1938, 5 T-26B tanks and no German tanks)

The Agrupación de Carros de Combate del Ejército del Sur, set up at the beginning of 1937 to be equipped exclusively with armoured material captured from the enemy, formed an FT-17 Tank Section in December of the same year, with tanks captured in the North, but these were gradually withdrawn from the front line. At the end of the war, the organisation chart of the Agrupación de Carros de Combate del Ejército del Sur was as follows:

- Command
- Tank Group
    - 2 Russian Tank Companies (with 9 T-26B each)
    - 1 FT-17 Tank Section (Renault FT-17)
    - 1 Company 'Negeillos' (temporarily added, with 11 Panzer I A)
- 1st Armoured Car Group
    - 1 Heavy Squadron (2 FA-1 and 8 BA-6)
    - 2 Light Squadrons (2 FA-1 and 8 UNL-35 each)
- 2nd Armoured Car Group:
    - 1 Heavy Squadron (2 FA-1 and 8 BA-6)
    - 2 Light Squadrons (2 FA-1 and 8 UNL-35 each)
- Workshop Unit

The unit had some other armoured vehicles (1 BT-5, 1 Hispano Suiza with T-26B turret and other unidentified armoured vehicles) and other vehicles (1 'Sadurní de Noya' tractor, 1 KhPZ Komintern tractor, etc.). At the end of 1938, the 2ª Agrupación de Carros de Combat was also formed, assigned to the Army of the South and also equipped entirely with material captured from the enemy. It was structured on:

- Command
- Tank Company (on 10 T-26B tanks and 3 Bilbao armoured cars)
- Light armoured car section (out of 9 UNL-35s and 2 Bilbaos)
- 1st Armoured Car Squadron (out of 8 BA-6 and 3 FA-1)
- 2nd Armoured Car Squadron (out of 9 BA-6 and 4 FA-1)

▲ Lieutenant Tamariz leads his company of five Italian-supplied light tanks as they enter San Sebastian on 15 September 1936. In the background of the photograph, taken on Calle Loyola, the Cathedral of the Good Shepherd (Tallillo) can be seen.

▼ To identify the war wagons captured by the Nationalists, the colours of the Spanish flag were placed on the turrets.

▲ An AAC-1937 armoured car, a copy of the Russian BA-6 but of Spanish manufacture, and a T-26 of the Nationalist faction, both hit and blocked by enemy fire, at an unknown location in Spain; the armoured car has the turret of a T-26 tank (Crippa).

▼ A captured T-26 and a Panzer I employed by Nationalist soldiers.

▲ A Franchist soldier standing on top of a BT-5 war tank in Fuentes de Ebro in 1938.

▼ Three Soviet T-26 tanks captured by the Franchists in Yuncos, Toledo province, in November 1936 (Bundesarchiv).

▲A Republican T-26 blocked by enemy fire, surrounded by soldiers loyal to Franco: this tank, once repaired, will be used by the Nationalists against its former owners.

▼ Spanish and Moroccan nationalist troops with a damaged T-26 Republican tank captured in Torrejón de Velasco, near Madrid, during the Battle of Seseña, at the end of October 1936.

▲ Also on the T-26s captured by the Franchists were conspicuous Nationalist markings, to prevent them from being hit by friendly fire. In particular, one notices the Spanish flag and the Tercio (Tallillo) symbol.

▼ A crowd of onlookers look at this T-26 captured and displayed as wartime prey on Plaza de las Tendillas in Cordoba on Christmas Day 1936.

▲ A mixed Nationalist armoured unit, consisting of T-26 war wagons, a Befelhlswagen I (command wagon) and German-supplied Panzer I tanks at Cubas de la Sagra, near Madrid, in January 1939.

▼ A T26 with Nationalist colours in the turret during a combat break.

▲ Nationalist convoy of a captured Russian-made T-26 tank and a Panzer I in the Valencian Community area of Castellón in May 1938.

▼ A priest blesses a Franchist tank before entering combat.

▲ A large Spanish flag was painted on the turret of this BT-5 captured from the Republicans to make it recognisable as a 'friend' to Francoist troops.

▼ National and regular soldiers examine a newly captured Soviet-made Republican T-26B. Photo taken on the Madrid front in mid-1937.

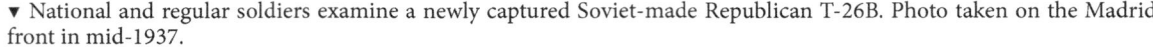

▲ A Russian tank depot captured from the Republicans (most are T-26s), sporting the Nationalist insignia (Hispanic Digital Library - CC BY-NC-SA).

▼ A T-26B parades through a Spanish city, led by soldiers loyal to Francisco Franco.

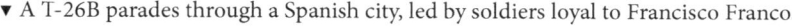

▲ Display of armoured vehicles and armaments captured from the Franchists by the Republicans: a T-26 tank and a BT-5 (Tallillo) tank are also present.

▼ Close-up of the T-26 tank from the previous photograph (Tallillo).

▲ Soviet-made T-26 tanks parade in a Spanish town at the end of the bloody Civil War (Tallillo).

▼ At the end of the Spanish Civil War, the tanks that had survived the conflict were integrated into the units of the reconstituted Spanish army, remaining on the line until the 1950s (Tallillo).

▲ These BA-6 armoured cars, photographed in 1950, ended their days with the Spanish Army in Sidi Ifni, Morocco.

▼ A T-26 of those used during the Spanish Civil War has survived to the present day and is preserved in the El Goloso Museum in Madrid. The vehicle, which appears here with a fanciful colour scheme, has recently undergone restoration and received a camouflage philologically in keeping with the period of its use.

Italian armoured units

Italian armoured units were initially part of the Spanish National Army, but later merged into the Italian Volunteer Troops Corps.

The first five CV33/35 assault tanks arrived at the port of Vigo in August 1936, accompanied by Italian instructors and specialists, who joined the Artillery Information Group (GIA) No. 3 based in Valladolid, forming a small tank unit called Grupo de Carros de Combate but actually little more than a Section, with Spanish crews and Italian technicians and instructors. The 'Group' was organised as follows:
- Command (1 command wagon)
- Tank section (4 tanks)
- Motor vehicle section
- Support section
- Repair team

With the arrival of 10 more tanks from Italy, the Italian-Spanish Tank and Artillery Group was formed and integrated into the Spanish Foreign Legion. The 1st Tank Company was organised on:
- 3 Platoons (4 tanks each)
- 1 Flamethrowing Tank Platoon (2 or 3 vehicles)

The Company participated in the advance on Madrid, distinguishing itself in the fighting around Navalcarnero on 21 October and was therefore named 'Compañía Navalcarnero'.

With the arrival of further supplies of CV33/35 tanks, a second company was established and on 22 December 1936 the two Tank Companies were transferred to the Volunteer Troop Corps; in the following January they took part in the Battle of Malaga.

On 11 February 1937, the Assault Tank and Armoured Car Grouping was created, with 5 Tank Companies, which merged a few days later into the Specialised Units Grouping, organised as follows:
- Command
- Tank Battalion on 4 Companies (each with 1 command tank and 3 Sections with 4 tanks)
- Armoured Car Company (8 Lancia 1Z and 1ZM)
- Motor Gunnery Company (3 Sections of 3 Motorcycle Squads)
- Flamethrower Company
- Anti-tank battery 47/32

In October 1937, the Special Forces Regiment was reorganised as the Carristi Regiment:
- 2 Tank Battalions (each on 2 Companies of 13 tanks)
- Motor Gunnery Company
- Armoured Car Company
- Flamethrower and Chemical Company
- Counter-Tanker Company
- Anti-Aircraft Company
- Engineer Company

The commander was Colonel Valentino Babini.

The Armoured Car Company, due to the small number and obsolescence of the Lancias it received, employed armoured vehicles captured from the enemy, eventually forming up with 6 Lancia 1ZMs,

1 BA-6 and 2 UNL-35s. Likewise, captured vehicles were incorporated into the Tank Battalion, which formed a Section of 5 T-26Bs, which was used on the Aragon front; 2 of those tanks, lost in combat, were replaced by 2 BT-5s.

In the autumn of 1938, the Carristi Regiment reached the following structure, which it maintained until the end of the Spanish Civil War:
- Command Company
  - Flamethrower Company
- 1st Assault Tank Battalion
- 2nd Assault Tank Battalion
- 3rd Motorised Battalion
  - Bersaglieri Company
  - Motor Gunnery Company
  - Armoured Car Company
- 4th Mixed Battalion
  - Flamethrower and Chemical Company
  - Mixed Anti-Tank Battery
  - Anti-Aircraft Company
  - Arditi Company
- Spanish Agrupacion
  - Command Company
  - Tank Company
- Repair and Recovery Centre
  - 2 reserve tank platoons.

Unfortunately, not even at the peak of the development of the Carristi Regiment did the Italian armoured units ever have the opportunity to prove their effectiveness as an organic and modern armoured unit: the Fast Tank Battalions were employed almost exclusively as infantry support, being split up between the different Divisions of the Volunteer Troop Corps.

▲ Soldiers of the Italian Carristi Regiment in Spain in front of a CV35 tank.

▲ Italian tanks during the Battle of Guadalajara: the first is a CV Flamethrower (BA).

▼ Republican soldiers pose around an Italian light tank captured during clashes in Guadalajara.

▲ Italian Lancia 1ZM armoured cars in a square in Malaga after the occupation of the city by the Nationalists; all armoured cars are painted grey-green.

▼ A CV35 on the move in a hilly location in Spain. On the vehicle are the tactical symbols adopted in the second half of the conflict, which should identify the 2nd tank from the 4th Company.

▲ Italian tanks along the Ebro river (Benvenuti - Colonna).

▼ Assault tank platoon at a halt. The tank crews adopt the one-piece turquoise tank crew suit, which will also be used throughout the Second World War.

▲ A CV35 tank and a T-26 captured and redeployed by the Carristi Regiment in Spain.
▼ CV33 on the march: the head gunner wears a protective leather jacket and helmet.

▲ A division of Blackshirts deployed in a pueblo watch a column of assault tanks of the Carristi Regiment pass by.

▼ Some assault wagons are prepared for transport by truck, to cope with a long journey. The trucks have the characteristic mottled camouflage adopted by the Volunteer Troop Corps' vehicles.

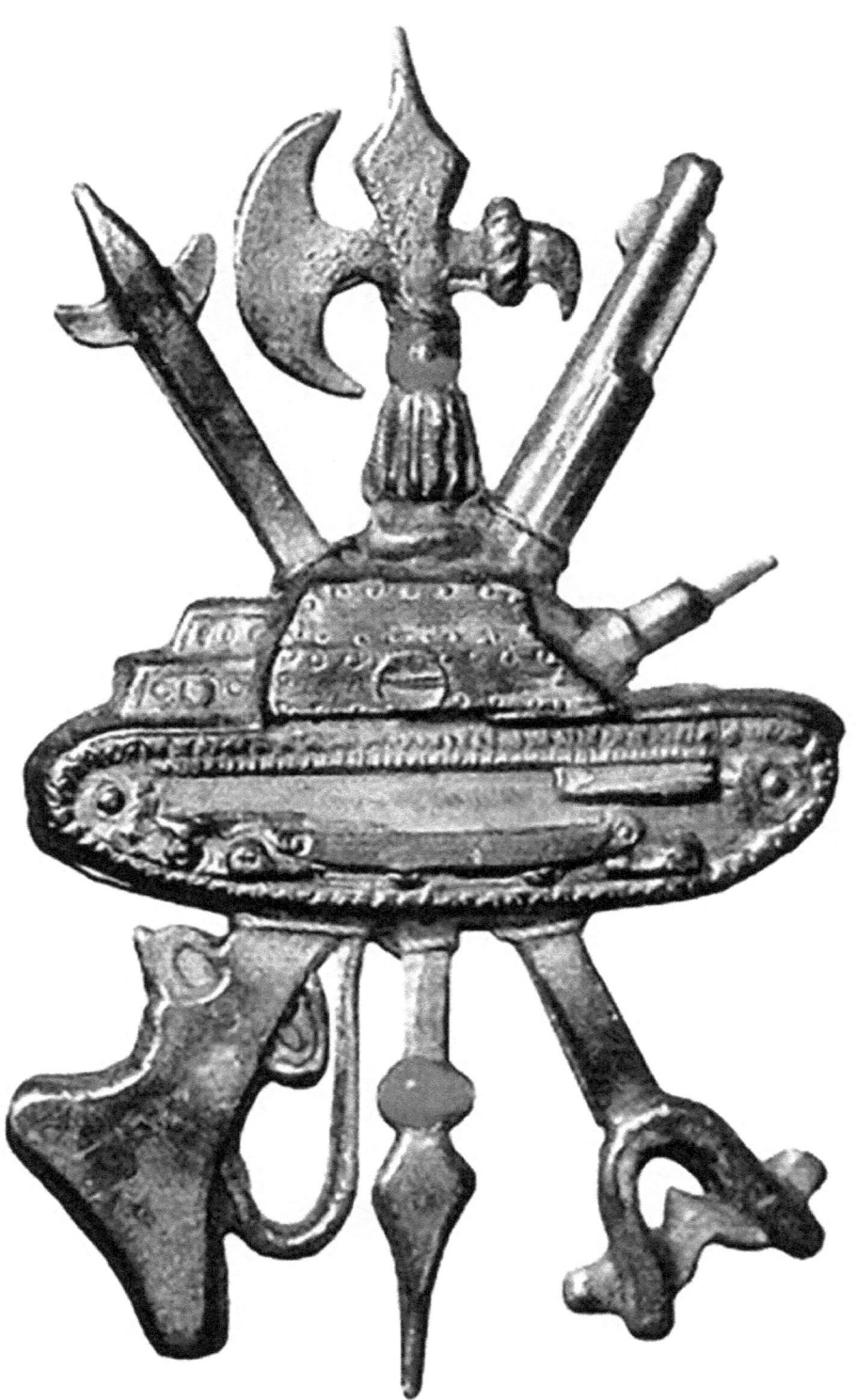

▲ Badge awarded to the soldiers of the Carristi Regiment, consisting of the badge of the Spanish Foreign Legion, charged with the silhouette of an Italian CV light tank.

▲ Republican armoured car, used by the Carristi Regiment.

▲ Light tank platoon deployed for a magazine. The second armoured vehicle from the right is a CV Flamethrower.

▼ An old Lancia 1ZM armoured car with the complex mottled camouflage adopted by the Volunteer Troops Corps for all wheeled vehicles, including the armoured cars of the Carristi Regiment.

▲ C.T.V. infantrymen with a CV33 assault tank, still bearing the old tactical symbols adopted in Italy from 1935.

▼ Platoon of four 1ZM lance armoured cars of the Carristi Regiment, including a command car with double turret. Although the photograph renders little, the original shows that they are all painted with the mottled camouflage pattern peculiar to the Spanish theatre.

▲ Major tank driver Paolo Lorenzo Paladini, commander of the 1st Assault Tank Battalion of the Volunteer Troops Corps, fell in Muniesa on 11 March 1938, while directing the action of his vehicles on foot. He distinguished himself particularly during the Spanish War and was decorated with a Gold Medal, three Silver Medals, three Bronze Medals for Military Valour and the Spanish Cross Laureate of San Ferdinando.

▼ An Ansaldo Lancia 1ZM armoured car on the outskirts of Málaga. The vehicle still appears to have a monochrome grey-green colour scheme.

▲ Italian assault tanks near Santander: on the CV33 in the foreground one can clearly see the mottled camouflage colouring, widely used on light tanks in those years.

▼ Italian Carristi surrounded by a cheering crowd in Santander.

▲ Chariots of the 2nd Company parade through the streets of Santander, immediately after the occupation of the city.

▼ A fast tank guards a square in Santander at the end of the clashes that led to the occupation of the city.

▲ The five Lancia 1ZM armoured cars still in operation in 1938 with the C.T.V.: two of them show obvious damage to the bodywork.

▼ In this photo, unfortunately of poor quality, one can see the stratagem adopted to strengthen the anti-tank defences of the fragile Italian light tanks: a 37 mm anti-tank gun was placed in tow, which was placed in firing position as needed by the crew members.

▲ A Soviet-made FAI armoured car, captured and used by the Volunteer Troops Corps (Tallillo),

▼ Some of the excellent blidno UNL-35s, produced in Spain, also ended up in the hands of the Volunteer Troops Corps units. Pictured here is one of these machines, captured by the 'Black Arrows' Division: a flashy Spanish tricolour was painted on the turret and the Division's motto, 'Agredir Para Vencer', was engraved on the casemate.

▲ Close-up of a Lancia 1ZM, still painted in grey-green.

▲ UNL-35 of the Carristi Raggruppamento: in the background can be seen a C.T.V. heavy truck, probably a Lancia RO.

▼ Italian infantrymen prepare for a firing action.

▲ Two UNL-35 armoured cars used by the Carristi Regiment, the distinctive camouflage colouring is quite evident.

▼ AAC-1937 armoured car, captured and re-used by the Italians, probably near Santander (Puddu).

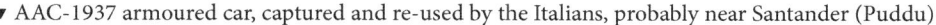

▲ This image allows us to appreciate the tactical symbols of the last type, adopted during the Spanish War: the semicircle in profile, on the side of the casemate, with the number 3, a number that was also repeated on the back of the casemate, indicating the number of the tank within the Company.

▲ An AAC-1937 armoured car captured from the enemy and redeployed by the Volunteer Troops Corps, photographed during the passage of a column of Italian logistics vehicles. The vehicle is followed by a Lancia 1ZM (NARA).

▼ Assault wagon with the fascio littorio on the side shield of the casemate. This symbol indicated the vehicle of the Battalion Commander (Puddu).

▲ Carrista Infantry Colonel Valerio Babini, commander of the Specialised Units Regiment, first, and the Carristi Regiment, then, from 25 April 1937 until 30 September 1938 (Puddu).

▼ Italian Carristi pay their respects to the drape of the Carristi Raggruppamento. The tank in the centre of the picture belongs to a Battalion Commander, as he has painted the fascio littorio on the sides of the casemate.

▲ Tanks of the Carristi Regiment enter a small town. It is interesting to note the numbering on the tank in the foreground on the right of the photograph, a vehicle that has a conspicuous camouflage with small patches, typical of the light tanks produced at the time. The wagon on the left, on the other hand, bears the symbol of the Battalion Commander (Puddu).

▼ Parade of Assault Chariots of the Carristi Regiment in Alicante on 31 March 1939 (Crippa).

▲ Section of Assault Tanks of the C.T.V. during the Barcelona review on 21 February 1939 (Lopez).

▼ On 19 May 1939, a Grand Review was held in Madrid, celebrating the Nationalist victory. The Raggruppamento Carristi hoisted a double Italian and Spanish flag during the Madrid Grand Revue (Benvenuti - Colonna).

German Armoured Units

Germany formed the 'Condor' Legion, consisting of ground and air units, to support Francisco Franco's troops. The German ground forces formed the 'Gruppe Imker':
- Imker Stab, command
- Imker Panzergruppe 'Drone', armoured group
- Gruppe Wolm, radio interception group
    - Imker Horch Kompanie
- Imker Ic, liaison and information section with the Generalissimo Headquarters
- Gruppe Imker Ausbilder, group of instructors in the Academies.

The Panzergruppe 'Drohne', commanded by Oberstleutnant Wilhelm von Thoma[1], was also known as Gruppe 'Thoma' and was equipped with tanks of the types PzKpfw I Ausf. A and PzKpfw I Ausf. B, consisting of four companies (the Group was also known as Pz.Abt. 88), which took part in the fighting, and a Flak unit, were used for both anti-aircraft and anti-tank defence. The unit had mainly organisational and training tasks; as seen above, using the material ceded to the Nationalists, a mixed Battalion was formed first and later a second. Both Battalions were placed under the 2nd Nationalist Tank Regiment. For the organisation of the units equipped with German tanks, please refer to the section 'Spanish Armoured Units', where the subject was dealt with in detail.

As far as armoured vehicles were concerned, the German High Command's interest in Spain was mainly oriented towards putting tactics into practice and testing new theories of Blitzkrieg and Von Thoma undertook to use Pz.Abt.88 for this purpose, supplementing its ranks with many T-26 tanks captured from the enemy. The Germans, in fact, were verifying the inadequacy of the Panzer I as a breakthrough tank, an experience that led to a review of the use of this tank family in infantry support, command and reconnaissance, while new tank designs (Panzer II, III, IV) were being developed in Germany.

---

[1] Wilhelm Josef Ritter von Thoma (Dachau, 1 September 1891 - Söcking, 30 April 1948) was placed in charge of the Armoured Group of the Condor Legion with the rank of lieutenant colonel. A great believer in the use of tanks and one of the pioneers of the armoured weapon after the First World War, Von Thoma was a frequent visitor to combat zones (for example, he personally led an armed assault on Madrid during the battle for the conquest of the city in November 1936). Later, during an interrogation by American soldiers at the end of the Second World War while he was a prisoner, the officer claimed to have directly participated in 192 war actions in Spain. After the end of the war, on 8 June 1939, von Thoma was assigned to Berlin as a staff officer. From 1 August to 18 September 1939, he was transferred to the Command of Panzer Regiment 3 of the 2nd Panzer Division and was later assigned to lead the regiment. Among his decorations are two very curious ones, which confirm that he was directly involved in battle on Spanish soil, the Cruz Española and the Medalla Militar.

▲ Germany contributed to the Nationalist cause by providing 96 PzKpfw I Ausf. A, 21 PzKpfw I Ausf. B, 4 Befehlswagen I (command tank) and 1 Panzer I without turret for instruction. Pictured are some Panzer Is that had just arrived in Spain, coloured in typical German feldgrau, still without any identifying markings.

▼ An officer and a tank driver of Panzergruppe 'Drohne', portrayed in front of a Panzer I, to which a Spanish flag was attached, to identify it as a Nationalist vehicle.

▲ At a later stage, some German tanks were given brown and, in some cases, brown and green mottled camouflage.

▼ Panzer I engaged in an impervious route. The panzer grey colouring earned the German tanks the nickname 'Negrilllos'.

▲ Deployment of the tanks of Gruppe Imker of the Legión Cóndor.

▲ With the passage of time, more complex identification signs, indicating the position of the individual tank in the department to which it belonged, and the symbol of the Tercio, the Spanish Foreign Legion, also appeared on German-made tanks alongside the nationality flag.

▼ German tanks on the Madrid front in 1936.

▲ Oberstleutnant Wilhelm von Thoma (right), commander of Panzergruppe 'Drohne', reviews his tank crew together with Generalfeldmarschall der Artillerie Walther von Brauchitsch.

▲ A Panzerbefehlswagen with the Nationalist insignia. The wagon, built on the hull of the light Panzer I Ausf. B., without turret, served as a command vehicle for the tank officers.

▼ A captured BA-6 armoured car (note on the turret doors the St. Andrew's cross used by the Nationalists) and a Panzer I of the 4th Company of Panzergruppe 'Drohne', photographed in Infiesto, Asturias, on 1 October 1937 (Bibliteca Nacional).

▲ A Panzer I, apparently still without Spanish markings, in the courtyard of a building hard hit by artillery shots: around the wagon Moroccan soldiers loyal to the Francoist cause.

▲ Infantrymen of Panzergruppe 'Drohne' lined up in front of some Soviet T-26 tanks.

▼ A ward of 'Negrillos' parked in the bush.

▲ Republican soldiers look curiously at this Panzer I knocked out by a shot that hit the casemate under the pilot's visor.

▼ Summer in Spain can be really hot, and these Panzergruppe 'Drohne' tank drivers wear clothes suitable for hot weather.

▲ Metal chest badge distributed to soldiers by the Panzergruppe 'Drohne': one can recognise typical elements of the symbolism of German armoured units.

▼ A group of German tanks parked in a clearing. From the left one can recognise a Panzer I rearmed with a Breda 20 mm machine gun, a Panzerbefehlswagen (painted entirely in panzergrau) and two Panzer I tanks.

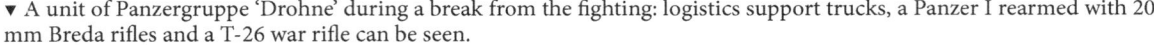

▲ On the sky of the casemate, next to the access hatch of this Panzerbefehlswagen, a conspicuous St. Andrew's Cross was painted, so that the vehicle could also be recognised by aerial reconnaissance.

▼ A unit of Panzergruppe 'Drohne' during a break from the fighting: logistics support trucks, a Panzer I rearmed with 20 mm Breda rifles and a T-26 war rifle can be seen.

▲ A Panzer I 'Negrillo' is loaded onto a truck for a long-distance transfer.

▼ During the Spanish conflict, some Panzer I were rearmed with an Italian Breda 20mm machine gun. In this image, a Panzer I Breda in charge of 3 Company: in the centre of the front shield is the coat of arms of the 'Tercio de los Etranjeros', while the meaning of the black letter 'E' in the centre of the rhombus is unclear, probably the initial of 'Especial', 'Special' (Cripɔa).

▲ The flag of the Legion Condor: the lower left-hand corner shows the symbol of the Phalange and the drape bears the yellow and red colours of Spain.

▼ Column of 'Negrillos' stopping in a Spanish town.

▲ German magazine dedicated to the armed forces in Spain. Flak units were incorporated into the Panzergruppe 'Drohne' with anti-tank and anti-aircraft functions.

▼ In this close-up of these two Panzergruppe 'Drohne' tank men, one can clearly see the insignia adopted on the black beret, later also adopted in the Second World War: the skull (also common to Panzer crews in the Second World War) and the swastika.

▲ A group of German infantry soldiers crowd around a German armoured column, opened by a Panzer I, on which the Tercio symbol stands out, and two T-26s captured from the Republicans.

▼ Thanks to the shot from this particular angle, one can clearly see the modifications made to the turret of this Panzer I in order to make the installation of the Breda 20 mm machine gun possible.

▲ Nationalist soldiers with an unconventional war prey (a pig) pose aboard a Panzer I armed with a Breda.

▼ A column of tanks from Panzergruppe 'Drohne' enters a Spanish town cheered by the crowd: a large national flag is raised on the Panzerbefehlswagen.

▲ In addition to the Panzerbefehlswagen command wagon, the column also consisted of at least four Panzer I tanks.

▼ At the end of the Civil War, numerous exhibitions of the war material used in the conflict were held: in this picture, a German Panzerbefehlswagen command wagon. (Tallillo)

▲ An SdKfz 265 Panzerbefehlswagen command car parades on Barcelona's Discord street during the 21 February 1939 parade (Tallillo).

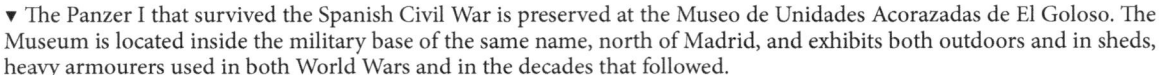

▲ A Panzer I of the reconstituted Spanish army participates in a parade in the immediate post-war period, raising a flag with the cross of St. Andrew (Tallillo).

▼ The Panzer I that survived the Spanish Civil War is preserved at the Museo de Unidades Acorazadas de El Goloso. The Museum is located inside the military base of the same name, north of Madrid, and exhibits both outdoors and in sheds, heavy armourers used in both World Wars and in the decades that followed.

REPUBLICAN ARMOURED UNITS

When the civil war broke out in 1936, these armoured units joined the Republican cause:
- Regimiento Ligero de Carros de Combate No. 1 (Renault FT17 and FT18 tanks)
- Gruppo de Autometralladores - Cannon (autoblindo Bilbao)
- Escuela Central de Tiro de Carabanchel

In total, the initial Republican armoured force thus amounted to 4 Schneider CA1 tanks, 9 Renault FT tanks, 1 FIAT 3000A tank (present at the Escuela Central de Tiro), 1 Trubia tank, 2 Landesa tanks and 41 Bilbao armoured cars: almost all Spanish armoured equipment had in fact ended up in Republican hands. The Schneider CA1s were used during the siege of the Alcázar of Toledo and the first defences of the capital Madrid.

This force was increased by the arrival from France of 3 Schneider tanks, which crossed the Catalan border on 9 August 1936, and some FT17 tanks, sent from Poland by sea. In fact, on 3 March 1937, 16 FT-17 tanks arrived in Valencia from Poland, 9 armed with 37 mm SA.-18 cannon and 7 with machine guns, which went to form a Company in the 1st Blindada Brigade. In 1938, the remaining FT-17s, probably 13 in number, were framed in the 'Agrupacion Renault', a de facto independent unit, but functionally answerable to the 2nd Brigada Blindada, based at the La Maddalena farm in Alcalà de Henares. The Agrupacion Renault was composed of:
- 1st Tank Section (command tank and 3 tanks), assigned to the 4th Division of II Corps, Villaverde, Madrid
- 2nd Tank Section (command tank and 3 tanks), assigned to the 7th Division of II Corps, San Fernando de Henares Sector
- 3rd Tank Section (command tank and 3 tanks), assigned to the 5th Division of II Corps, Alto de la Carrascosa sector
- 4th Tank Section (command tank and 3 tanks), assigned to the 5th Division of II Corps, Cerro Alto sector.

Starting in December 1937, the Republican FT-17s concentrated in the Agrupacion Renault were assigned to various Divisions until the end of the war, in particular to the 4th, 5th and 7th Divisions, in 4 Sections of 3 tanks, used for the defence of fixed positions along an essentially static front, without ever participating in any noteworthy operations. With the arrival of the Soviet T-26 tanks, the surviving FT-17s were effectively withdrawn and rarely participated in armed engagements. The Republicans also made use of homemade tanks and a large number of armoured trucks, called 'Tiznaos', a subject that will be dealt with in a later volume.

On 23 March 1937, the 'Euskadi' Light Tank Battalion was formed, which included a Trubia-Naval Company (tanks produced in Sestao, in the Basque Country) under the command of Captain Luis Basterretxea de Arendia; the tanks were numbered 7, 8, 9, 11 and 13 and were delivered to the crews on 29 March. On the following 5 April, the Battalion commander, Captain Carlos Tenorio Cabanillas, issued a fiery report, pointing out numerous shortcomings of this tank which include low engine power, insufficient adherence of the track to the ground, fragility of the clutch, low height of the mudguards from the ground, and an uncomfortable narrow fighting compartment.

On the same day, a Trubia-Naval on the Urquiola road destroyed a Nationalist 'tiznao', capturing a hill defended by the Condor Legion. On 7 April, Trubia-Naval number 12 was lost in a fight against the Nationalists; on the 27th, due to the Nationalist advance, the Trubia-Naval Company retreated to Durango/Yurreta, 26 km from Bilbao, where it was reinforced with some BA-6 armoured cars.

Throughout May, the Trubia-Naval were divided between different units and sent to cover retreating infantry units, which fell back to Bilbao. On 3 June, some Trubia-Naval took part in the assault against Peña Lemona, managing to recapture the high ground, but suffered with five crew members wounded; on the 17th the tanks were used again in action to cover a retreat. When the general retreat from Bilbao was ordered the next day, the Trubia-Naval tanks defended the city centre while the town was evacuated. When the Nationalists arrived on 19 June, the Trubia-Naval Company managed to escape and retreated towards Santander.

At the beginning of July, all available Trubia-Naval were sent to Laredo, headquarters of the Northern Army Tank Regiment, and by 6 August, the Trubia-Naval were incorporated into the Republican Army, as the Basque region had fallen. In all, only one Trubia-Naval vehicle had been lost since March in the entire Biscay campaign. On 10 August, the Trubia-Naval tanks were divided into two sections, one sent to cover the Reinosa road and the other to Olea, to defend against the Nationalist advance on Santander. Not many details are known about the use of the tanks at Santander, but it can be assumed that they were again used to cover the retreat. On the 14th, an unknown number of Trubia-Naval and Renault FTs were sent to the Escudo pass in support of a section of BA-6s and FAIs, allowing the Soviet vehicles to retreat. Some would be used two days later at Reinosa. On 26 August, the defenders of Santander surrendered to the Italian C.T.V. forces and four Trubia-Naval tanks were captured; allegedly, one tank was held with the intention of sending it to Italy for study, although it is not possible to confirm whether this actually happened.

After the capture of Santander and the collapse of the Republican Army of the North, the Nationalists directed their efforts on Gijón, where the Republican armoured forces consisted of a Renault FT Battalion, a Trubia-Naval Battalion and some armoured cars. Due to the fierce resistance of the Republican militia, the Nationalist advance was slow and, due to the uneven terrain, the use of tanks was limited, although on 20 October a Trubia-Naval and a Renault FT were captured at Infiesto, on the Oviedo-Santander railway. With the fall of Gijón on 21 October, the so-called 'War of the North' came to an end and the surviving armoured vehicles ended up in Nationalist hands. However, the Republican armoured units saw a greater expansion after the supply of armoured vehicles by the Soviet Union, which began in September 1936 and ended in early 1938. In fact, Stalin saw an opportunity in the Spanish Civil War to create a communist state loyal to Moscow on the border with France and consequently authorised the sending of armaments and armoured vehicles. In total, the USSR sent about 60 BA-6 armoured cars, about 400 BA-10 armoured cars, 281 T-26B tanks and more than 50 BT-5 fast tanks to Spain. Together with the armoured vehicles, tank specialists were also sent as instructors, but, due to the lack of experience of the Republicans, at first the crews of the tanks sent into combat were made up of Soviet tank commanders and drivers and Spanish gunners. A period of training was necessary so that gradually the Republican tank crews were formed almost exclusively by Spanish personnel, starting at the end of 1937.

Shortly after the arrival of the first Russian tanks in Spain, in Archena, the 1st Tank Battalion was organised, with three Companies of 3 Platoons, each with 3 tanks; in November 1936, the 2nd Battalion was organised and by December, the 1st Armoured Brigade was formed, with three Battalions of T-26B tanks in all a total of 96 tanks. In the spring of 1937, the Brigade grew to 4 Tank Battalions and an Reconnaissance Company with BA-6 armoured cars; in the same period, the 2nd Armoured Brigade was also formed, with a similar composition.

In June 1937, 4 independent Tank Battalions, equipped with T-26Bs, assigned to each Army to provide armoured support to infantry divisions, and 3 tiznaos (each with 3 Companies of 10 vehicles each), grouped in the so-called Auto-armoured Regiment (sometimes also referred to as the Auto-armoured Brigade), were also operational. In September 1937, a Heavy Tank Regiment was formed, equipped with 48 BT-5s, organised into 3 Battalions of 2 Companies, with 2 Platoons each.

In October 1937, the Armoured Division also referred to as the Armoured Engineer Division, was formed, consisting of 2 Armoured Brigades (T-26B), the Heavy Tank Regiment (BT-5), 1 Infantry Brigade and 1 Artillery Company.

Commander of the Republican Armoured Forces was Colonel Sanchez Perales, who in 1938 implemented a reorganisation of the armoured units. The Republican Armed Forces found themselves divided in two and in April 1938, the 1st Armoured Division, assigned to the Army Group East, and the 2nd Armoured Division, assigned to the Army Group of the Centre, were created. The Regimiento de Carros Pesados BT-5 remained in charge of the 2nd Armoured Division[2].

▲ A FIAT 3000 tank, which was in service at the Escuela Central de Tiro in Madrid. The tank, which had been acquired in 1924 for evaluation tests, took part in the first actions of the Republicans in Madrid, but its fate during the conflict is unknown (Juan Antonio Luceno).

2 Consulting various sources, there is much confusion about the Republican armoured units at the end of the war. The two Divisions formed in 1938, for example, are often referred to as Brigades. In addition, numerous small armoured Groups and Platoons were created and attached to the various Armies into which the Republican front was divided. To follow the organisational development and operations of these units in detail would require an entire monograph, so it has been decided to outline only the main lines here, and it is beyond the scope of this text to go into the subject in detail.

▲ The same wagon on the cover of the Republican magazine 'Estampa' of 1 May 1937, in an image that probably refers to an exercise held before the war.

▲ A Soviet BT-5 tank: tanks of Soviet origin adopted an identification number, painted white, as their only identifying mark.

▼ A BT-5 survivor of the Spanish Civil War, photographed in the 1970s.

▲ In this unfortunately poor quality image we see a Renault FT-17 tank of the Regimiento de Carros No. 1 being unloaded from a truck for use in action in the Guadarrama area on 27 July 1936.

▼ A Schneider CA1 wagon on the calle Santa Fe in the Alcazar of Toledo, 20 or 21 September 1936 (Agencia EFE).

▲ The same wagon of the previous photograph was blocked by a mechanical failure, as Luis Quintanilla recounts in his book 'The Hostages of the Alcázar of Toledo': *'The metal monster continued its pursuit through the narrow alleyway leading to one of the gates of the Gobierno Militar, and, when it was almost reaching it, its old engine broke down, remaining there unusable until the end of the siege'*.

▲ On this Schneider CA-1 were handwritten numerous phrases praising the different movements that made up the Republican front.

▼ The Soviet BT-5 fast tanks were the heaviest modern tanks that participated in the Spanish conflict. In this photo, a Republican BT-5 in fast movement on an Iberian road.

▲ Republican armoured cars near Oviedo in 1937.

▼ A republican BA-6 heavy armoured car abandoned in the city centre of Santander after the occupation by the Francoists.

▲ At the end of the clashes in Santander, the Nationalists sent the captured armoured vehicles by rail to a number of metal industries, so that they could be restored to fighting condition. The photo shows a Renault FT-17, at least one Trubia tank and a BA-6 armoured car.

▼ A 1933 model T-26 knocked out during the Battle of Teruel, in a photograph taken in December 1937.

▲ Soviet t-26 tanks moving through the snow during the Battle of Teruel (December 1937 - February 1938).

▼ Nationalist troops in Teruel advance towards the bullfighting arena, leaving abandoned Republican tanks behind.

▲ A Republican wagon captured by the Nationalists on the Aragon front.

▼ Republican armoured trucks (called 'tiznaos') on the Aragon front.

▲ A Republican UNL-35 armoured car in Aragon: this locally produced vehicle was one of the best products of the Iberian war industry.

▼ An old Renault FT-17 stationed in the park of a small Spanish town, camouflaged with some branches.

▲ This unique armoured car of Portuguese origin also took part in the Spanish Civil War with the Republicans.

▼ The famous American writer Hernest Hemingway interviews the crew of a Republican tank. Hemingway, who participated in the conflict as a war correspondent in the ranks of the Republican army, based his novel 'For Whom the Bell Tolls' on his personal experience in Spain during the Civil War.

▲ Italian legionaries from the Volunteer Troops Corps overtake an abandoned Republican tank.

▼ FAI armoured car painted entirely in green.

▲ A German soldier inspects the interior of a knocked-out Republican FT-17 tank.

▼ The contribution made by the Soviet BT-5 tanks to the Republican cause was unfortunately limited by the inexperience of the Republican soldiers (Tallillo) due to their poor ability in armoured vehicle combat.

▲ A group of boys and children curiously observe a T-26.

▲ A Russian soldier studies the effects of enemy fire on this disabled FT-17.

▼ A BA-6 of the Republican People's Army. This Soviet armoured car served as a model for the construction of the AAC-1937, which was built in Spain by local factories.

▲ The exhausted crew of a T-26 photographed aboard their tank, together with other Republican soldiers (Tallillo).

▲ With the passage of time, the tactical signs on Republican chariots became more articulated, although the symbolism adopted is not clear (Tallillo).

▼ A Republican tank, which had been sent to reinforce the troops deployed at Brunete, remained on the battlefield at the end of the fighting (Tallillo).

▲ A BA-6 arrived in Madrid to help defend the city in November 1936.

▲ Although the BT-5 was the most technologically advanced and modern vehicle used in the Spanish Civil War, its poor tactical use, as demonstrated at Fuentes del Ebro, sealed its fate (Tallillo).

▼ A Soviet-made KhPZ Komintern tractor, captured by the Nationalists during the Battle of Brunete (Tallillo).

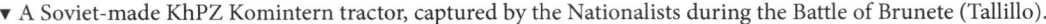

▲ Republican tank officer photographed in front of his tank.

▼ A T-26B in 1938, photographed as it prepares to cross the Ebro river.

▲ Fleeing Spanish Republican units reach the French border at Le Perthus with their own armoured vehicles.

▼ Despite its tactical misuse and the numerous losses it suffered from its first deployment, the T-26 proved to be superior to any other tank used in battle.

▲ A Renault FT-17 tank photographed in Plaza de Neptuno in Madrid.

▼ A T-26 is inspected by the Nationalists at the end of a fight (Tallillo).

▲ Many Soviet tanks, especially T-26s, were captured virtually intact by the Volunteer Troop Corps and were thus redeployed against their previous owners (Tallillo).

▼ For long-distance travel, the Republican tanks were transported on special trailers.

▲ In 1938 in the city of San Sebastian there was a large exhibition of weapons captured by the Nationalists from the 'Reds' during the Civil War. Among them was this Renault FT-17, probably of Polish origin.

▼ The replica of a Russian BA-6 armoured car preserved in Spain at the Museum of the Battle of the Ebro in Fayon.

▲ Uniform of a Soviet tank officer in Spain.

▲ A Schneider heavy cart in Madrid, near the Royal Palace.

▼ A Scheider manoeuvred by soldiers of the Republican faction.

▲ A Republican supply column escorted by a T-26 approaches the town of Brunete in July 1937.

▼ A 1933 model T-26 Republican tank with volunteers from the 11th International Brigade during the Battle of Belchite in 1937.

▲ A Franchist officer poses next to a Russian heavy tank, taken from the Republicans, on which was written the eloquent phrase: 'Captured from the Reds in the Flentes sector'.

▼ On this Renault Republican wagon you can see the white numerical identification system.

BIBLIOGRAPHY

BOOKS

- Albert P.C. , "Carros De Combats Y Véhiculas Blindados de la Guerra 1936-1939", Borras Ediciones, 1980.

- Ales Stefano, Viotti Andrea, "Le uniformi e i distintivi del Corpo Truppe Volontarie Italiane in Spagna 1936-1939", U.S.S.M.E., Roma, 2004.

- AA.VV., "Storia dei mezzi corazzati", Fratelli Fabbri Editore, Milano, 1976.

- Barlozzetti Ugo, Pirella Alberto, "Mezzi dell'Esercito Italiano 1935 – 1945", Editoriale Olimpia, Firenze, 1986.

- Benvenuti, Colonna "Fronte Terra – Carri Armati Vol. 2/I" – Edizioni Bizzarri.

- Benvenuti, Colonna "Fronte Terra – Carri Armati Vol. 2/II" – Edizioni Bizzarri.

- Barlozzetti Ugo, Pirella Alberto, "Mezzi dell'Esercito Italiano 1935 – 1945", Editoriale Olimpia, Firenze 1986.

- Battistelli Pier Paolo, Cappellano Filippo, "Italian Light Tanks 1919 – 45", "New Vanguard" n° 191, Osprey Publishing, Oxford (U.K.), 2012.

- Gianni Bianchi, Del Giudice Davide, "Hombre sin medo - Uomo senza paura", Associazione Culturale Sarasota, Massa, 2011.

- Capodarca Valido, "Immagini ed evoluzione del Corpo Automobilistico", volume I (18989 – 1939), Comando Trasporti e Materiali dell'Esercito, Roma, 1994.

- Cappellano Filippo, Pignato Nicola, "Gli autoveicoli da combattimento dell'Esercito Italiano", volume I, S.M.E. – Ufficio Storico, Roma, 2002.

- Ceva Lucio, Curami Andrea, "La meccanizzazione dell'Esercito fino al 1943", U.S.S.M.E., Roma, 1989.

- Chiappa Ernestino, "C.T.V. – Il Corpo Truppe Volontarie italiano durante la Guerra Civile Spagnola 1936 – 1939", E.M.I., Milano 2003.

- Crippa Paolo, "Carristi italiani in Spagna 1936 – 1939", Mattioli 1885, 2022.

- Falessi Cesare, Pafi Benedetto, "Veicoli da combattimento dell'Esercito Italiano dal 1939 al 1945", Intryama, Bologna, 1976.

- John F. Coverdale, "I fascisti italiani alla guerra di Spagna", Laterza, Roma - Bari, 1977.

- Mortera Perez Artemio, "Los medios blindados en la guerra civil española: Teatro de operaciones del Norte 36/37", AF Editores, Valladolid (E), 2007.

- Mortera Perez Artemio, "Los medios blindados en la guerra civil española: Teatro de operaciones de Andalucía y Centro 36/39", AF Editores, Valladolid (E), 2010.

- Mortera Perez Artemio, "Los medios blindados en la guerra civil española: Teatro de operaciones de Levante, Aragón y Cataluña 36/39", 1° volume, AF Editores, Valladolid (E), 2013.

- Mortera Perez Artemio, "Los medios blindados en la guerra civil española: Teatro de operaciones de Levante, Aragón y Cataluña 36/39", 2° volume, AF Editores, Valladolid (E), 2013.

- Parri Maurizio, "Tracce di cingolo", Associazione Nazionale Carristi d'Italia – Sezione di Verona, Verona, 2106.

- Petacco Arrigo, "Viva la muerte! Mito e realtà della guerra civile spagnola 1936-1939", Arnoldo Mondadori Editore, Milano, 2006.

- Pignato Nicola, "Dalla Libia al Libano", Editrice Scorpione, Taranto, 1989.

- Pignato Nicola, "Motori!!! Le truppe corazzate italiane 1919 – 1994", GMT, Trento, 1995.

- Pignato Nicola, "Un secolo di autoblindate in Italia", Mattioli 1885, Fidenza (PR), 2009.

- Puddu Mario, "Carristi d'Italia in terra di Spagna", Tipografia Artistica Nardini, Roma, 1965.

- Quintanilla Luis, "Los rehenes del Alcázar de Toledo", Ediciones Espuela de Plata, Spagna, 2015.

- Riccio Ralph, Pignato Nicola, "Italian Truck-Mounted Artillery in action", Squadron Signal Publications, Carrolton (U.S.A.), 2010.

- Rovighi Alberto, Stefani Filippo "La partecipazione italiana alla guerra civile spagnola (1936 – 1939)", Ufficio Storico Stato Maggiore dell'Esercito, Roma, 1992.

- Tallillo Antonio, Tallillo Andrea, Guglielmi Daniele "Carro L3 – Carri veloci, carri leggeri, derivati", G.M.T., Trento, 2004.

- Tallillo Antonio, Tallillo Andrea, Guglielmi Daniele, "Carro FIAT 3000 – Sviluppo, tecnica, impieghi", G.M.T., Trento, 2018.

- Tavoletti Francesco, "Gli scudetti da braccio italiani 1930 – 1946", Edizioni FT, Milano, 2000.

- Zaloga Steven, "Spanish Civil War Tanks – The proving ground for Blitzkrieg", Osprey Publishing, Oxford (U.K.), 2010.

ARTICLES

- AA.VV., "Estampa" n° 484, anno X, Madrid, 1° maggio 1937,

- AA.VV., "Italiani in Spagna" in "Prospettive" n° 6, 2ª edizione, Edizioni di Prospettive, Roma, 1938.

- Cattarossi Emanuele, "Carristi italiani in Spagna – L'occasione mancata" in "Quaderni" n°1/2004, Società di Cultura e Storia Militare.

- Ceva Lucio, "Ripensare Guadalajara" in "Rivista Storica Italiana", Fascicolo II, 1992.

- Dominique Renaud, "Carro de combate ligero Verdeja n°1", in "TNT" n° 43, maggio – giugno 2014.

- Yann Mahé, "No Pasaràn, une guerre mécanisée improvisée", in "Batailles et Blindés" n° 36, aprile – maggio 2010.

- Laurente Tirone "Mad Max en Espagne! Les matérieles du camp républicaine", in "TNT" n° 39, settembre – ottobre 2013.

- Manrique J.M., "Algo más sobre los "carros italianos" en la Guerra de España (36 – 39)" -1ª parte in "Historia Militar", Maggio 2000.

- Manrique J.M., "Algo más sobre los "carros italianos" en la Guerra de España (36 – 39)" -2ª parte in "Historia Militar", Luglio 2000.

- Manrique J.M., "Algo más sobre los "carros italianos" en la Guerra de España (36 – 39)" - 3ªparte in "Historia Militar", Settembre 2000.

- Montanari Mario, "L'impegno italiano nella guerra di Spagna" in "Memorie storico – militari", U.S.S.M.E., Roma, 1980.

- Tocci Patrizio, "Le autoblindo Lancia 1ZM" - 3ª parte in "Storia Militare" n° 69, Luglio 1999.

- Tomasoni Matteo, Grassia Edoardo, De Renis Alice, Bottoni Gaia, "Agredir Para Vencer – L'inno della Divisione Mista Frecce – Un documento inedito della Guerra Civile Spagnola" in "Diacronie - Studi di Storia Contemporanea" n° 12/4 – 2012.

OTHER DOCUMENTS

- Colonnello Babini Valerio, "Relazione sulle operazioni da Rudila (9 marzo) a Tortosa (19 aprile 1938)", Raggruppamento Carristi – Comando.

Acknowledgements

The publication of my first research work was made possible thanks to two people, who believed in me and my modest literary skills. They are Luca Cristini of Soldiershop - Luca Cristini Editore, who gave me this opportunity, and Paolo Crippa, director of the "Witness To War" series, who introduced me to the world of military publishing, giving me precious information and ideas, useful to set up, start and finish the drafting of this first book, which will surely be affected by many flaws, due to inexperience. I must also thank him for granting me the use of photographs from his archive and some extrapolated plates from his book 'Italian Carristi in Spain 1936 - 1939', which also served as a basis for the drafting of the chapter on Italian Carristi military units, employed during the Civil War in the Iberian Peninsula.
My thanks also go to Antonio Tallillo, the talented author of numerous monographs on Italian tanks, who kindly provided me with numerous images that appear in this volume.
Finally, I apologise in advance for any errors, omissions, inaccuracies, particularly due to the unfamiliarity I have with writing for readers, this being my first editorial work.

The author

TITOLI GIÀ PUBBLICATI - TITLES ALREADY PUBLISHING

BOOKS TO COLLECT

www.ingramcontent.com/pod-product-compliance
Lightning Source LLC
LaVergne TN
LVHW070523070526
838199LV00072B/6685